I0762820

You will never know how much it cost
the present generation to preserve your freedom!
I hope you will make a good use of it.

—John Adams

★ ★ ★

Heroes of 1776

The STORY OF the DECLARATION of INDEPENDENCE

★ ★ ★

For America's children.

As you turn these pages, we hope you see the promise of liberty our Nation holds for you—and the courage it takes to defend it. —NMG & JN

AUTHORS' NOTE

In writing about heroes of the past, separating myth from fact can be no small task. Did John Hancock sign boldly so the King wouldn't need spectacles to read his name? Did Charles Carroll worry about being confused with a relative? Did Caesar Rodney ride entirely on horseback or take a coach part of the way the night of July 1? Did a British shot really lodge in the floorboards by Elizabeth Lewis's feet? When, exactly, did Deborah Hart die, and what were Nathan Hale's precise final words? In truth, no one knows. What we can say is the stories we relate here are very old and have become part of the fabric of our nation's history. It is in that spirit that we share them. In doing so, we have sought to rely as much as possible on primary accounts—on the memoirs, letters, and autobiographies of the signers—or on other eighteenth- and nineteenth-century source material, including biographies the signers' descendants wrote. When quoting from original sources, we have at times standardized grammar, capitalization, and style choices. We have done so solely in the interest of readability and without intent to change substance. We are grateful to the authors who have come before us and preserved for future generations the stories of courage and sacrifice that we tell here.

HarperCollins Children's Books, a division of HarperCollins Publishers, 195 Broadway, New York, NY 10007

HarperCollins Publishers, Macken House, 39/40 Mayor Street Upper, Dublin 1, D01 C9W8, Ireland

Heroes of 1776: The Story of the Declaration of Independence

Samuel Adams portrait by John Singleton Copley, courtesy of the Library of Congress; Thomas Paine portrait by Peter Kramer, courtesy of the Library of Congress; The Declaration of Independence, courtesy of the National Archives; Mary Katharine Goddard print line, Library of Congress, Rare Book and Special Collections Division, Continental Congress & Constitutional Convention Broadsides Collection; William Franklin, Governor of New Jersey portrait, from The New York Public Library; Benjamin Franklin portrait by Joseph Siffred Duplessis, The Friedsam Collection, Bequest of Michael Friedsam, 1931; James Armistead Lafayette portrait, attributed to John B. Martin, Collection of the Valentine Museum

harpercollins.com

Library of Congress Control Number: 2026930747
ISBN 978-0-06-347397-3

The artist used acrylic paint on paper to create the illustrations for this book.
Designed by Rick Farley and Jon Corby
26 27 28 29 30 PC 10 9 8 7 6 5 4 3 2
First Edition

Heroes of 1776

The Story of the Declaration of Independence

By Neil Gorsuch
and Janie Nitze

Illustrated by Chris Ellison

HARPER
An Imprint of HarperCollinsPublishers

In the spring of 1776, Philadelphia buzzed with the sounds of revolution. Men and women stopped each other in the streets to trade rumors of the latest troop movements. Others whispered reports about spies among them. Noisy debates spilled from open tavern windows while distant drums called soldiers to their training.

WHICH SIDE WOULD YOU CHOOSE?

By some estimates, around 15 to 20 percent of American colonists were loyalists. Another 40 percent or so were patriots. The rest supported neither side. With the stakes so high, picking a side took courage. For many, the safest path was to remain neutral.

What sparked this talk of revolution? "Patriots" were fed up with British rule. They bitterly opposed laws that forced colonists to house British troops, open their homes to searches by British agents, and endure trials before royal judges rather than local juries. Perhaps most of all, patriots opposed taxes imposed on them by far-off rulers rather than their own elected leaders. They wanted instead a new Nation where the people would rule themselves and laws would protect the rights of individuals to live, speak, and worship freely.

But even now, not everyone agreed. Yes, British troops and American colonists had already exchanged shots in battle. But many "loyalists" wanted to avoid more conflict and hoped the colonies could patch up their differences with Great Britain.

KING GEORGE III (1738–1820)

King George III clung to the colonies as sources of wealth and global power and paid close attention to the growing rebellion. But the rebels weren't his only interest: "Farmer George," as he was affectionately known in Britain, enjoyed working in his fields and gardens and supported new farming techniques. Sadly, as his mind unraveled later in life, he took on a new nickname: "The Mad King."

Philadelphia served as an important meeting spot in 1776. And it was where all 13 colonies sent delegates to represent their views and debate their collective future in a Continental Congress.

The delegates met nearly every day in the State House's assembly room. Benjamin Franklin, the celebrated inventor, was there. So were Thomas Jefferson and John Adams, both future presidents. A pair of firebrands from Massachusetts, John Hancock and Samuel Adams, arrived together but led very different lives. Hancock was one of the colonies' richest men and enjoyed fine clothes, food, and wine. Adams, meanwhile, scorned luxury and lived frugally. So frugally that his friends felt compelled to give him a new, more respectable set of clothes for his first trip to Philadelphia.

SAMUEL ADAMS (1722–1803)

The British thought Samuel Adams so dangerous that, knowing he was poor, they tried to bribe him to abandon his revolutionary ways. When in 1775 the British offered to pardon colonists who renounced the patriot cause, only two men were excluded from the offer: Samuel Adams and John Hancock. Their offenses the British deemed too villainous to pardon.

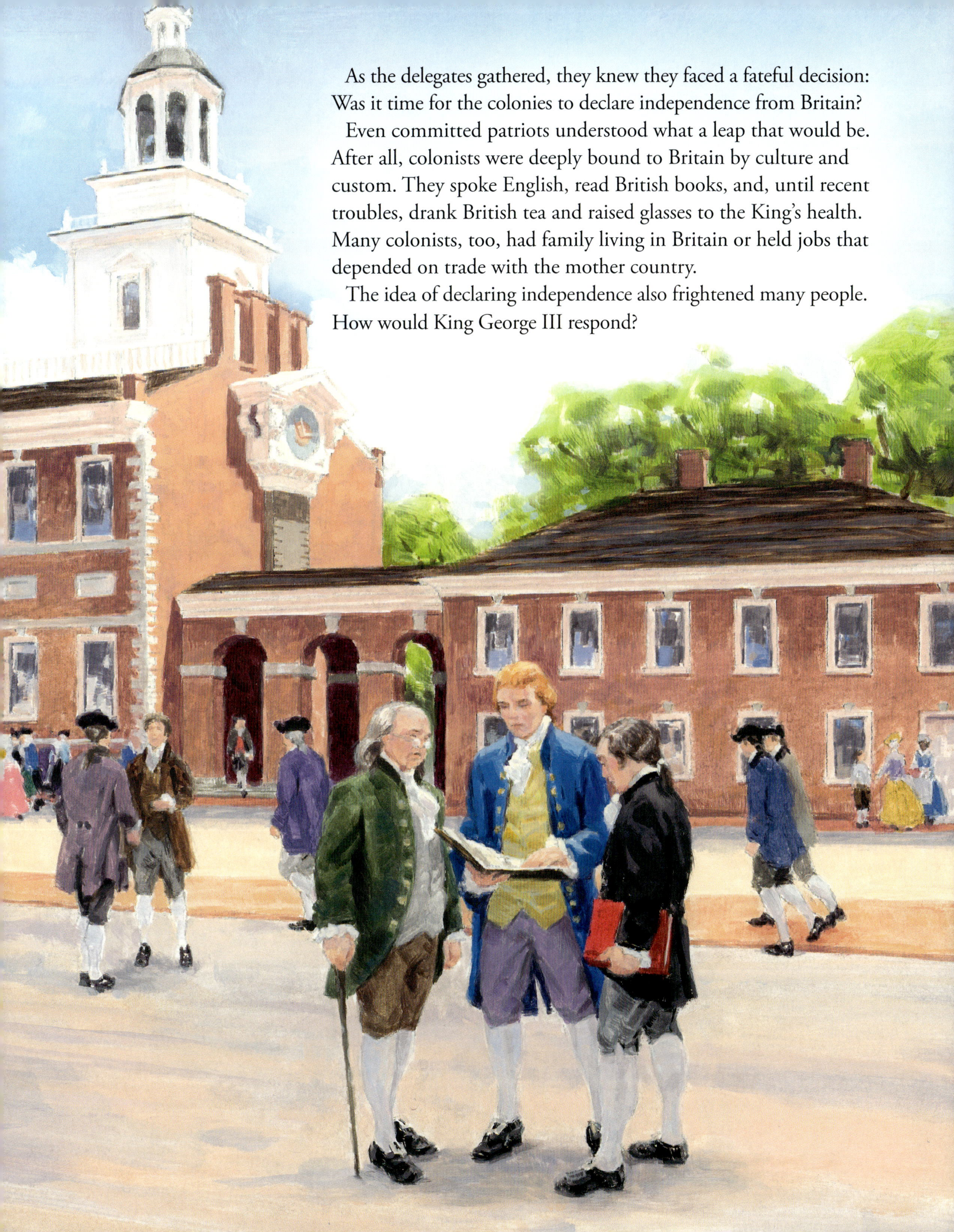

As the delegates gathered, they knew they faced a fateful decision: Was it time for the colonies to declare independence from Britain?

Even committed patriots understood what a leap that would be. After all, colonists were deeply bound to Britain by culture and custom. They spoke English, read British books, and, until recent troubles, drank British tea and raised glasses to the King's health. Many colonists, too, had family living in Britain or held jobs that depended on trade with the mother country.

The idea of declaring independence also frightened many people. How would King George III respond?

There was good reason to fear the King. Britain had the world's most powerful navy—more than 200 warships—and a large army that had won many battles around the globe. Its soldiers were well trained and well supplied with muskets, ammunition, and backpacks filled with blankets and clothes.

In April 1775, as British troops marched on Lexington and Concord, Massachusetts, many believed they sought not only to seize the patriots' stash of weapons but also to capture Samuel Adams and John Hancock. On the night of April 18, Paul Revere and William Dawes rode from Boston in part to warn them of the advancing British troops.

Making fun of the red coats British troops wore, some colonists called the soldiers "lobsters." But in truth, those well-stitched uniforms only showed how ragged the colonies' forces were by comparison. The Continental Army and local militias—groups of ordinary citizens ready to defend their hometowns and colonies—included farmers and laborers. Many had never set foot on a battlefield and lacked basic supplies like food, uniforms, even shoes.

As John Adams wrote, "Our army [is] not so strong as we could wish. The militia . . . not so ready as they ought to be."

Still, Adams thought it was time to declare independence. Richard Lee of Virginia agreed, and on June 7, he asked the delegates to adopt this resolution:

"That these United Colonies are, and of right ought to be, free and independent States."

The resolution divided the men. Unable to agree and feeling the gravity of the decision, they decided to continue deliberating and put off any vote until July 1.

Meanwhile, to prepare a Declaration of Independence in case they decided to vote for one, the delegates appointed a committee of five men from different colonies: Benjamin Franklin of Pennsylvania, John Adams of Massachusetts, Roger Sherman of Connecticut, Robert Livingston of New York, and Thomas Jefferson of Virginia, the colony with the largest population.

The men all respected each other, but they had to decide: Who would take the pen?

Years later, Adams recounted how he and Jefferson answered that question. Jefferson insisted to Adams: "You ought to do it."

Adams replied: "I will not."

"Why?"

"Reasons enough."

"What can be your reasons?"

"Reason first," Adams answered. "You are a Virginian, and Virginia ought to appear at the head of this business. Reason second. I am obnoxious, suspected, and unpopular. You are very much otherwise. Reason third. You can write ten times better than I can."

"Well," Jefferson concluded, "if you are decided, I will do as well as I can."

Jefferson wrote the Declaration in a little over two weeks. A book lover who in time built a library of over 6,000 volumes, he later said that he "turned to neither book or pamphlet," but aimed simply to compose "an expression of the American mind." Working in rooms he rented from a bricklayer on the city's edge, Jefferson rarely spoke in the larger assembly. "During the whole time I sat with him in Congress," John Adams once remarked, "I never heard him utter three sentences together."

The Declaration Jefferson produced wasn't very long. After some changes from the other delegates, it was shorter than many letters (about 1,300 words). Yet it was radical. It didn't just declare the colonies to be "Free and Independent States." It offered a timeless and universal declaration of human liberties:

> **"We hold these truths to be self-evident, that all men are created equal, that they are endowed by their Creator with certain unalienable Rights, that among these are Life, Liberty and the pursuit of Happiness.—That to secure these rights, Governments are instituted among Men, deriving their just powers from the consent of the governed."**

Those words proclaim three big ideas:

First, "all men are created equal." The rich and the poor, the popular and the unpopular: all are equal in God's eyes and should be equal under law.

Second, each person enjoys rights—among them life, liberty, and the pursuit of happiness—that are God-given. Those rights are "unalienable," beyond the reach of government.

Third, to preserve those rights, the people have another right: the right to rule themselves. The government exists to serve the people, not the other way around.

Old Europe was stunned. The idea that *all* men are equal? Have God-given *rights*? Should *rule* themselves? These weren't just radical ideas; they were deeply dangerous to Europe's kings and nobles. Many Britons reacted with anger, dismissal, or scorn. One British magazine scoffed that Americans had claimed "an unalienable right of talking nonsense."

Often shy in public, Thomas Jefferson loved the natural world. He cultivated vegetable gardens at his home, kept dogs and mockingbirds as pets, and for a time even had a pair of grizzly bear cubs. His favorite mockingbird, named Dick, had a special cage suspended in the window of his study. When alone, Jefferson would open the cage and let Dick fly around the room or perch on his shoulder, even take food from his lips. Dick was "the constant companion of his solitary and studious hours," his friend once observed. "How he loved this bird!"

On July 1, decision day, the delegates packed into the assembly room. The morning was hot and humid. Horseflies from a nearby stable stole through the open windows and bit the men's legs. The delegates rose in turn to give long speeches for and against independence.

By the evening, only 9 of the 13 colonies voted for independence. South Carolina and Pennsylvania voted "no." Delaware's delegates were tied 1 to 1. And while New York's delegates favored independence, they were unable to vote for lack of instructions from home.

One of South Carolina's delegates, Edward Rutledge, moved to retake the vote the next day. He had opposed independence but now set about persuading his delegation to vote for it. As he saw things, it was more important for the colonies to stand united than for his own personal views to prevail. Overnight, South Carolina became a "yes."

In the meantime, Thomas McKean of Delaware sent an urgent message to Caesar Rodney—a fellow delegate home on military business—urging him to ride to Philadelphia to break Delaware's tied vote.

John Adams once described Rodney as "the oddest-looking man in the world," tall and thin with a face "not bigger than a large apple." Rodney suffered from a cancer that left his face marred with scars; by the end of his life he took to hiding it behind a green silk scarf. A true patriot, some say he had refused to travel to Britain for perhaps his best chance at a cure.

Rodney received McKean's message during a violent thunderstorm but knew he couldn't wait for better weather. He leaped on his horse and rode 80 miles through the night with the rain lashing his sides.

The next day, July 2, Rodney staggered into the assembly room, still soaking and caked in mud but in time to vote for independence. Delaware was now a "yes."

What about Pennsylvania? The day before, its delegation had voted against independence 4 to 3. Yet today, two of Pennsylvania's seats sat empty. Like Rutledge, those two delegates knew how important it was for the colonies to stand together. By avoiding the assembly, they allowed their delegation to vote for independence by the slimmest of margins: 3 delegates to 2. Now, Pennsylvania was a "yes."

That left only New York. Its delegates still hadn't received instructions from home, so they declined to vote at all. The final tally? 12–0. (Soon after, New York also voted for independence, making the decision unanimous.)

John Adams wrote to his wife, Abigail, that on that day, "the greatest question was decided which ever was debated in America, and a greater perhaps never was or will be decided among men."

THOMAS PAINE (1737–1809)

Thomas Paine, a poor British man who arrived in the colonies in 1774, did perhaps as much as anyone to fuel the patriot cause. In January 1776, he anonymously published a thin pamphlet called *Common Sense*, making a passionate case for independence. The work became an instant bestseller. George Washington called its reasoning "unanswerable." Paine could have become rich from the sales. Instead, he donated his profits to the Revolution and, in the words of a biographer, "gave away a fortune in that pamphlet alone."

After the vote, the delegates turned to the draft Declaration. For two days, they discussed and reworked the document. Finally, on July 4, the delegates agreed on a final version.

Now every hour mattered. Facing long odds against a powerful empire, the delegates knew their chances of success would shrink further if news of the Declaration didn't reach their fellow colonists quickly. So the delegates sent riders carrying freshly printed copies to each of the 13 colonies.

The effect was electric. A ripple of joy radiated from Philadelphia as the news spread. Eager crowds gathered in town after town to hear local leaders read the Declaration aloud. People cheered, rang church bells, and lit bonfires in celebration.

George Washington, commander of the Continental Army, received word while in New York City. Eager to inspire his troops for the battles to come, he ordered the men to assemble. As the Declaration was read out loud, soldiers broke out in whoops of joy. Later, swept up in the spirit of the moment, a mob wielding ropes and axes stormed a 4,000-pound statue of King George III that stood at the southern tip of the city. Flinging ropes over the statue, the group tore it down and hacked off the head. Patriots planned to display it on a spike. But, before they could do so, some say loyalists stole the head and shipped it to Britain.

Still, the patriots made good use of the rest of the statue. Composed of lead, most of it was sent to Connecticut to be melted down and turned into musket balls—more than 42,000 of them. Now, one colonist wryly wrote to a friend, British troops "will probably have melted Majesty fired at them."

Thomas Jefferson wasn't happy with all of the delegates' changes to his careful drafting. "Mutilations," he called them. Benjamin Franklin tried to cheer him up with a story. There was a hatmaker, Franklin said, who planned on opening a shop and putting up a sign with an image of a hat and the words: "John Thompson, Hatter, makes and sells hats. For ready money." Pleased with his sign, the hatmaker showed it to some friends. The first complained that the word "hatter" was unnecessary. A second criticized the word "makes" as pointless too. A third struck out "for ready money," pointing out that customers expect to pay for hats, after all. So now the sign read simply, "John Thompson sells hats." But then other friends did away with the words "sells" and "hats," arguing that the image of a hat said all that. So, Franklin told Jefferson, "the sign was reduced ultimately to 'John Thompson,' with the figure of a hat."

Back in Philadelphia, many of the delegates gathered on August 2 to sign the Declaration. This time, the assembly room wasn't filled with debate. It was silent. Every delegate knew that by adding his name to the page, he was committing what the British would consider an act of treason—a crime punishable by death.

One delegate later wrote to John Adams: "Do you recollect the . . . awful silence which pervaded the house when we were called up, one after another . . . to subscribe what was believed by many at that time to be our own death warrants?" "The silence and the gloom" were interrupted only when a heavy delegate turned to a skinny one and boasted that, when the British hanged them all, he would at least have the advantage of dying quickly. Meanwhile, his skinnier friend would "dance in the air an hour or two."

John Hancock of Massachusetts, president of the assembly, went first. His bold, oversized signature is impossible to miss. Legend has it he wrote large enough to make sure the King could see his traitorous act without spectacles.

Stephen Hopkins of Rhode Island signed his name very differently. His signature is smaller and wobblier. But that isn't because he lacked courage. Hopkins suffered an illness that made his hands shake. Usually, he let others write for him, but today he wanted to do it alone. "My hand trembles," he announced as he signed, "but my heart does not!"

As Maryland's delegates were called one by one, Charles Carroll approached the desk. John Hancock asked if he would sign. "Most willingly," Carroll replied. When someone remarked that his common name might shield him from British vengeance, Carroll added to his name "of Carrollton," his hometown, declaring, "They cannot mistake me now!"

The final line of the Declaration underscored the delegates' resolve:

"For the support of this Declaration, with a firm reliance on the protection of divine Providence, we mutually pledge to each other our Lives, our Fortunes and our sacred Honor."

★ ★ ★

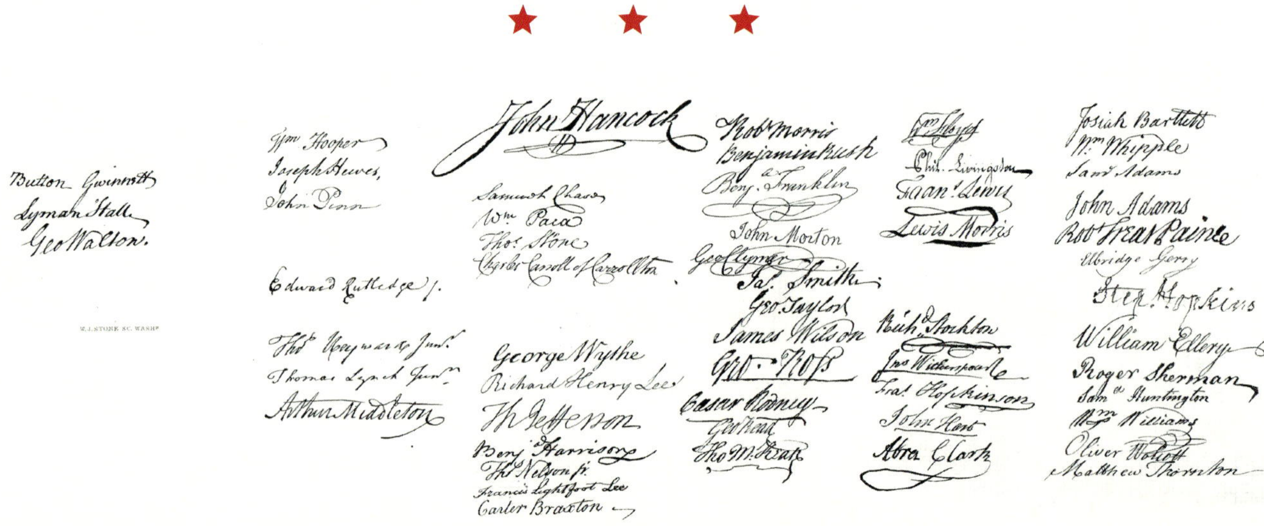

Later, to print the Declaration with the signers' names, the delegates turned to Mary Katharine Goddard. A patriot well-known to the delegates, she had taken over her younger brother's newspaper and turned it into a voice of resistance.

Typically, Goddard printed her newspaper under the name "M. K. Goddard." But on the Declaration, she did something different. She wrote her full name at the bottom:

BALTIMORE, in MARYLAND: Printed by MARY KATHARINE GODDARD.

Perhaps she, too, wanted the world to know she dared to stand on the side of freedom—no matter the cost.

The Declaration of Independence ignited a full-scale war with Britain. And as the Revolution's most visible leaders, the delegates had marked themselves as special targets for the King's vengeance.

Soon after the signing of the Declaration, British troops marched on the home of New York signer Francis Lewis. His wife, Elizabeth, was home. When a shot struck the floorboards by her feet, she didn't budge but defiantly declared: "Another shot is not likely to strike the same spot." Soldiers stormed the house, destroyed many of the family's belongings, and arrested Elizabeth. She was imprisoned under brutal conditions. By the time of her release, her health was gone and she soon passed away. Francis Lewis, grief-stricken, died years later. By then, only a fraction of his once-large fortune remained, his family observing that "the greater part of it [was] spent in the service of the country."

Another signer, Richard Stockton, left Philadelphia to help the army. He found the troops in need of almost everything. A "great part of the men" are "barefooted and barelegged," he wrote to a fellow delegate. "My heart melts with compassion for my brave countrymen who are thus venturing their lives in the public service, and yet are so distressed." Stockton helped find shoes and clothing for the soldiers—he even donated his own stockings—before returning to his duties as a delegate.

Later, as the British invaded his home state of New Jersey, Stockton rushed back to protect his family. He moved his wife and children some 30 miles away for safety and then took refuge with a friend. Soon, though, loyalists found where he was hiding, dragged him from bed, and locked him in prison. Near-starved and cold, Stockton was shattered when he was released months later. By then, the British had destroyed his property and set fire to his prized library, one of the finest in the colonies. Stockton was left with little to his name and died a few years later. He never saw the end of the Revolution to which he had given so much.

THE FRANKLIN FAMILY. The war tore many families apart. Benjamin Franklin's only son, William (left), remained loyal to the Crown, worked to undermine the Revolution, and eventually retreated to Britain. For years, father and son hardly spoke. "Nothing has ever hurt me so much and affected me with such keen sensations," Franklin (right) wrote to William in 1784, "as to find myself deserted in my old age by my only son; and not only deserted, but to find him taking up arms against me, in a cause wherein my good fame, fortune, and life were all at stake."

John Hart of New Jersey, too, was a marked man. After he returned home from Philadelphia, his wife, Deborah, fell gravely ill and died. As British forces closed in on his farm, Hart fled for the woods.

In the dead cold of winter, Hart eluded British patrols. He hid in caves and cottages and never dared to sleep in the same place twice. Once, he spent a bitter night curled up next to a dog. Despite a promise from the British that they would pardon any rebel who retracted his support for independence, Hart stood firm.

He, too, never lived to see the end of the Revolution. A fellow signer wrote of him: "A plain, honest, well-meaning Jersey farmer, with but little education, but with good sense and virtue enough to discover the true interests of his country."

As the Revolution wore on, one signer after another suffered. The British captured at least five over the course of the Revolution. One lost his son in the war. Abraham Clark of New Jersey had not just one but two sons captured by the British. One was brutally confined in a dungeon, left to starve except for scraps of food other prisoners stuffed through the keyhole of his cell.

In the end, about a third of the signers saw their homes damaged or destroyed. Nearly all were left poorer for their dedication to the cause of freedom.

The Revolution dragged on for years, and often the patriots teetered on the edge of defeat. Washington lost one battle after another. For a time, there was even talk of replacing him as commander of the army. Despite support from so many colonists, patriot soldiers regularly lacked muskets, food, even clothing. "I am now convinced," Washington wrote early in the war, "that unless some great and capital change suddenly takes place . . . this army must inevitably be reduced to one or other of these three things. Starve—dissolve—or disperse."

Still, the patriots refused to give up. "These are the times that try men's souls," wrote Thomas Paine. "Tyranny, like hell, is not easily conquered." Eventually, too, the patriots won some key battles, and the fledgling Nation convinced France to enter the war as an ally. With France's vast resources, many hoped the tide of the war would turn.

Then, in 1781, Washington saw his chance. British general Charles Cornwallis had stationed his army at Yorktown, Virginia, near the mouth of the York River, awaiting the arrival of British ships. But before they could reach him, Washington struck. His army attacked by land while French warships blocked escape by sea. Trapped, Cornwallis surrendered on October 19, marking the end of the last major battle of the war.

Yorktown was the hometown of one of the signers, Thomas Nelson, Jr., and he joined in the fight as commander of the Virginia militia. Legend has it that, on learning that British troops were stationed in his home, he didn't hesitate to order his men to fire on it.

Victory did nothing for Nelson's personal fortunes. He died in 1789 a poor man, his once-great wealth spent on the patriot cause. Before he died, Nelson was asked if he felt bitter about his fate. "I would do it all over again," he replied.

Who were these men who risked their lives, fortunes, and sacred honor for freedom? Not professional soldiers. Some were merchants, others farmers. About half were trained in the law. Many would have been better off under British rule; they could have enjoyed comfortable lives amassing power and wealth under the King.

In their sacrifice, the signers were not alone. The colonists didn't win freedom because they were richer or smarter or better supplied. They won in large measure because of the daily acts of courage and sacrifice of thousands of ordinary men, women, and children.

Across the 13 colonies, men joined groups like the Sons of Liberty to resist British rule. Farmers donated crops, blacksmiths hammered out weapons, and carpenters built forts. Some men joined local militias, ready to mobilize at a moment's notice. Others enlisted in the army when doing so promised little but hunger and disease. "You might have tracked the army . . . by the blood of their feet," Washington said about one long winter march, because so many of his soldiers had to walk barefoot or with feet wrapped in rags. Some men became spies, too. A young Nathan Hale volunteered to spy for the Continental Army but was caught by the British. Facing death bravely on the gallows, Hale reportedly offered these final words: "I only regret that I have but one life to lose for my country."

JAMES ARMISTEAD LAFAYETTE (ca. 1748–1830)

Black Americans, both free and enslaved, sacrificed greatly for the patriot cause, even though the Declaration's promise of equality did not yet extend to them. Some took up arms in the Continental Army, others fought in local militias. Nurses and cooks, carpenters and blacksmiths contributed too. Some, like Phillis Wheatley, wrote poetry inspired by the Revolution. Others, like James Armistead Lafayette, served as spies. A double agent, Lafayette both passed false information to the British and gathered intelligence vital to George Washington at the Battle of Yorktown. Over a century would pass before many historians began to recognize and celebrate these Americans' efforts.

Women formed their own resistance groups like the Daughters of Liberty. Many wives ran farms and businesses to keep their families afloat while their husbands fought. Others sought to choke off British trade by refusing to buy imported goods. Thousands of women traveled with the army, too, enduring hardships alongside the men while helping to cook, mend clothes, and tend to injured soldiers. Some joined in battle. Deborah Sampson Gannett dressed as a man and served for over a year in Washington's army before being discovered. Mary Ludwig Hays, on the battlefield to deliver water to the troops, seized her wounded husband's cannon to fire at the enemy.

Children contributed too. With parents focused on war responsibilities, children often took on many of their jobs, tending livestock, harvesting crops, or helping to keep shops open and running. Other children served in the Continental Army and local militias as drummers and fifers. Some served as spies and messengers, hoping they might avoid suspicion thanks to their youth. One of them, 18-year-old Emily Geiger, volunteered to ride through enemy territory and deliver a message to a patriot general. When the British captured her midway through her journey, she quickly memorized the message and swallowed the paper on which it was written. Then she fled and rode on.

After many long and exhausting years of war, the American people finally won the Revolution and faced the difficult task of building a new Nation founded on the Declaration's ideals.

In 1788, they again put aside their differences and came together as one to ratify the Constitution. The Constitution created a new national government with limited and divided powers, one in which the people are not mere subjects but sovereign, with the right to choose their own leaders.

Three years later, the American people added the Bill of Rights to further protect individual liberties like the freedoms of speech and religion and the right to trial by jury.

Two of the signers of the Declaration, John Adams and Thomas Jefferson, became the second and third presidents of the new Nation. They didn't always agree. Adams favored a strong central government, while Jefferson believed that individual liberties were best protected by states and local authorities. Their rivalry got so heated that for over a decade the two stopped talking to each other.

Yet later in life they set aside their disagreements. "You and I ought not to die before we have explained ourselves to each other," Adams wrote to Jefferson. In the same spirit of unity that brought about the Declaration and Constitution, they became friends again.

In all, the pair went on to exchange over 150 letters, many of them reflecting on the events that had led to the Revolution. "A letter from you calls up recollections very dear to my mind," Jefferson wrote to Adams. "It carries me back to the times when, beset with difficulties and dangers, we were fellow laborers in the same cause, struggling for what is most valuable to man, his right of self-government."

The two men, who had devoted their lives to the cause of freedom, died just hours apart on the same day: July 4, 1826, the 50th anniversary of the adoption of the Declaration of Independence.

Jefferson's health had been declining for years, and by late June he could hardly rise from bed. Yet his mind remained clear. Sensing his end was near, he penned a final letter, declaring: "All eyes are opened, or opening, to the rights of man."

On July 3, Jefferson slipped in and out of sleep, waking briefly in the evening to whisper, "Is it the Fourth?"

He drew his final breath a little past noon the following day.

That same day, John Adams, frail and nearly blind, woke to the sound of bells ringing. Asked if he knew what day it was, he answered: "Oh yes. It is the glorious Fourth of July. God bless it. God bless you all."

At some point, a group of visitors asked him to supply a toast for use in that day's public celebrations. Adams answered them: "I will give you: Independence forever."

A few moments of silence passed. Someone present asked Adams if he might like to add anything. Adams's eyes brightened.

"Not a word."

ESS. JULY 4, 1776.
States of America.

A MESSAGE FROM NEIL GORSUCH

Why did my dear friend Janie Nitze and I write this book? After all, many other books about the Declaration of Independence exist. What could we possibly add?

A touch of humanity—at least that is our hope. It wasn't simply a series of events—the Stamp Act, the Boston Massacre, the Battles of Lexington and Concord—that led to the Declaration and the founding of our Nation. At the heart of it all were ordinary people willing to do extraordinary things and risk all they had to secure a better life for themselves, their children, and generations to come.

As Janie and I finish writing this book, the Nation is poised to celebrate the Declaration's 250th anniversary. Today, that document is one of America's most cherished historical treasures. Over one million people make the trip every year to see it at the National Archives in Washington, DC. The Constitution may establish our form of government, but it is the Declaration that expresses America's ideals: Self-rule. Equality. God-given rights, including the rights to life, liberty, and the pursuit of happiness.

The men, women, and children who helped found our Nation in 1776 suffered greatly for those ideals.

But the truth is, the work is never done, and the torch passes to each new generation to defend the Declaration's ideals and to help make our Nation truer to them still.

When Elizabeth Cady Stanton and her colleagues gathered in Seneca Falls, New York, in 1848 to argue for equal rights for women, they appealed to the Declaration, insisting that "all men *and women* are created equal."

Years later, as Americans plunged into civil war, Abraham Lincoln called on the country to abolish slavery. It should have no place, he argued, in a Nation dedicated to the idea that *all* of us are created equal. America, Lincoln believed, needed to "come back to the truths that are in the Declaration of Independence."

Standing before the Lincoln Memorial in Washington, DC, in 1963, and addressing continued racial discrimination in our society, Dr. Martin Luther King, Jr., invoked the Declaration once more: "I have a dream that one day this nation will rise up and live out the true meaning of its creed: We hold these truths to be self-evident, that all men are created equal."

The Declaration has inspired freedom movements not just in America but across the world. In 1776, our new republic stood almost alone. Today, nearly half the world's population lives in some form of democracy, and many countries have declarations modeled on our own.

What will be the Declaration's next chapter? Respect for individual rights, equal treatment of all people, and democratic self-government do not just happen. They require courage and hard work to defend in every generation. As Frederick Douglass said: "Stand by [the Declaration's] principles, be true to them on all occasions, in all places, against all foes, and at whatever cost." The torch is now in your hands.

Neil Gorsuch